Compact School and College Administrator's Guide for Compliance with Federal and State Right-To-Know Regulations

Chemical and Environmental Safety and Health in Schools and Colleges Series

Compact School and College Administrator's Guide for Compliance with Federal and State Right-To-Know Regulations

Written Hazard Communication Program for Schools and Colleges

Concise Manuals of Chemical and Environmental Safety in Schools and Colleges

Volume 1   Basic Principles
Volume 2   Hazardous Chemical Classes
Volume 3   Chemical Interactions
Volume 4   Safe Chemical Storage
Volume 5   Safe Chemical Disposal

Pocket Guides to Chemical and Environmental Safety in Schools and Colleges
(Five condensed, portable versions of the *Concise Manuals*, with the same volume numbers and titles as above)

Handbook of Chemical and Environmental Safety in Schools and Colleges

Compendium of Hazardous Chemicals in Schools and Colleges

List of Lists of Worldwide Hazardous Chemicals and Environmental Pollutants

Cross-Reference Index of Hazardous Chemicals, Synonyms, and CAS Registry Numbers

Index of Hazardous Contents of Commercial Products in Schools and Colleges

Compact School and College Administrator's Guide for Compliance with Federal and State Right-To-Know Regulations

THE FORUM FOR SCIENTIFIC EXCELLENCE, INC.

Science Information Resource Center

J. B. LIPPINCOTT COMPANY
PHILADELPHIA

Cambridge / New York / St.Louis / San Francisco
London / Singapore / Sydney / Tokyo

ISBN 0-397-53023-4

Foreword to the Series

The Forum For Scientific Excellence, Inc. (FSE) has spent many years developing an integrated hazardous chemical management program for schools and colleges. This program is the result of careful consideration of all existing regulatory requirements at federal and state levels, practical experience and awareness of actual needs within the educational environment, and the best ideas from employee committees and management teams. As our on-the-job experience in schools and colleges has revealed new informational needs, we have expanded the available resources.

This comprehensive school and college series has been designed to benefit administrators and employees alike. In order to effectively modify poor employee work habits, often established over the course of many years, employees must be provided with hazardous chemical information in a variety of continuous, complementary ways that will remind them that their health and safety on the job depend on personal knowledge and work practices. Simultaneously, management needs to become more aware that safety and health on the job raises productivity and morale. Administrators should implement not only "bare minimum" procedures, but also a responsible hazardous chemical management program that fulfills all three of the following objectives:

1. *Public Responsibility*: What must be done to properly protect employees, students, or contractors who work in an educational facility, and maintain public confidence.
2. *Tort Liability*: What can be done to minimize the potential for lawsuits.
3. *Regulatory Compliance*: What the laws require.

We have found that educational institutions often have neither enough time nor money to do the job right the first time, but always have enough time *and* money to do it over—after there has been an accident, lawsuit, or fine. Similarly, employees often "know a better way," even if it is *not* safer, until there is an accident on the job. Then they often retort: "*You* should have *made* me listen!"

Two books in this series have been designed specifically to increase the knowledge and awareness of school and college administrators:

Compact School and College Administrator's Guide for Compliance with Federal and State Right-To-Know Regulations

Written Hazard Communication Program for Schools and Colleges

Ten employee training manuals have been designed to progressively increase employees' knowledge and awareness of hazardous chemicals:

Concise Manuals of Chemical and Environmental Safety in Schools and Colleges

Volume 1	*Basic Principles*
Volume 2	*Hazardous Chemical Classes*
Volume 3	*Chemical Interactions*
Volume 4	*Safe Chemical Storage*
Volume 5	*Safe Chemical Disposal*

Pocket Guides to Chemical and Environmental Safety in Schools and Colleges (condensed editions of the five volumes listed above)

Five reference books have been developed to give both administrators and employees in schools and colleges access to identification, properties, and hazard information for chemicals and products:

Handbook of Chemical and Environmental Safety in Schools and Colleges (consolidates all the information in the *Concise Manuals* into one major reference)

Compendium of Hazardous Chemicals in Schools and Colleges

List of Lists of Worldwide Hazardous Chemicals and Environmental Pollutants

Cross-Reference Index of Hazardous Chemicals, Synonyms, and CAS Registry Numbers

Index of Hazardous Contents of Commercial Products in Schools and Colleges

Although we have applied considerable experience and expertise in the development and integration of this hazardous chemical management system, customized adjustments within your school or college should probably be considered to cover any special local needs or conditions. Specific state or institutional regulations or priorities also may warrant some modifications in this system, but we have tried to accommodate as many contingencies as we could envision.

The breadth and depth of the Series will certainly leave considerable opportunity for improving areas in each book. We invite comments and suggestions that will improve these publications for all potential users.

Dr. George R. Thompson, CEO
The Forum For Scientific Excellence, Inc.

Contents

APPENDIXES

Introduction

The Compact School and College Administrator's Guide provides a synopsis of requirements your school or college must implement in order to comply with the OSHA Hazard Communication Standard as well as applicable state right-to-know (RTK) laws. It has been prepared by The Forum For Scientific Excellence, Inc. (FSE) to help administrators understand more readily the legal, regulatory, and liability issues involved in hazardous chemical management responsibilities. This Guide is intended to facilitate development of an efficient and effective compliance program, as well as to provide more responsible safety and health capabilities within schools and colleges.

Detailed regulatory requirements may be obtained directly from the regulations, the OSHA office nearest you, your responsible state agency, various school or college associations, or independent consultants.

We have incorporated sample letters, formats, and outlines in the Appendixes to help you understand the full spectrum of compliance requirements and to simplify your compliance efforts. These attachments include both informational sources for your consideration and resources for your direct use.

Many of the suggestions and ideas recommended here were developed following practical experience in the hundreds of schools and colleges we have serviced and advised since

1985. Some of the recommendations in this book are not specifically required by the regulations, but represent practical solutions that we have developed to existing, real needs at the request of many school and college administrators. The suggestions should prove helpful to you in implementing your program.

Employer Guidelines

The Occupational Safety and Health Administration (OSHA) regulation governing hazardous chemicals in the workplace was originally promulgated as a Final Rule in 1983 for chemical manufacturers (SIC Codes 20-39), but did not become effective until November 25, 1985, because of various challenges within the courts. On August 24, 1988, the OSHA Hazardous Communication Standard was expanded under a federal appellate court mandate to include *all employers* in the United States.*

As a result of this ruling, schools and colleges in 23 states and 2 territories with OSHA-approved state plans (Table 1) must provide information to their employees through Material Safety Data Sheets (MSDSs), training programs (written and/or oral), and labels. The philosophy behind this regulation is based upon employees' "right to know" information concerning hazardous chemicals to which they may be potentially exposed. This OSHA health and safety standard requires that the hazards of all chemicals produced or imported by chemical companies be fully evaluated. It also

---

*On May 20, 1988, the 1st Circuit Court of Appeals stayed the May 23, 1988, implementation of the expanded standard for all nonmanufacturing employers. This stay was lifted on June 24, 1988, for all nonmanufacturing employers except the construction industry.

comprehensively addresses the issue of other employers' evaluating their chemical hazards and communicating this information to their employees.

The OSHA Hazard Communication Standard can be found in Title 29 of the Code of Federal Regulations (CFR) in Subpart 2 of Part 1910, specifically at 1910.1200. These regulations delineate the hazard determination process and criteria, define the required content of MSDSs, and describe the necessary scope of training and written hazard communication programs. The broad extent, as well as the detailed specificity, of these requirements not only render historic MSDSs obsolete, but also necessitate new management initiatives, policies, and procedures to assure that your school or college fully complies within the required deadlines.

Individual right-to-know laws and regulations have been enacted by 18 states (Table 2). Only 9 states and the District of Columbia neither have individual state right-to-know laws nor comply with the OSHA Hazard Communication Standard (Table 3). (Several local governments, including Cincinnati and Philadelphia, have also passed right-to-know ordinances, but these local regulations will not be discussed in this book.) Foresight and planning will enable you to comply simultaneously with federal, state, and local right-to-know requirements with a single hazard communication program.

The responsibilities inherent in either the OSHA Standard or the individual state Right-To-Know laws (Table 4) encompass only eight specific areas, plus some unique requirements, although not every set of hazardous chemical regulations involves each of these areas. A comparison of the federal and state regulations indicates both the common and the unique requirements (Table 5). Of the 18 state and 1 federal set of regulations, 17 include a hazardous substance list. Inventories, audits, or surveys are required by 18 of 19, but the specific content and the reporting requirements vary among the regulations. Chemical and/or product research is required by 18 of 19 to assure that the employer recognizes and understands the chemicals or product components that require hazard communication to employees. Hazardous chemical data sheets are required by all 19 regulations, with 17 of 19 relying upon MSDSs from the manufacturer. New Jersey and New York have chemical data sheets (but *not* product data sheets) available for employers within their states. Hazard assessments are required only by OSHA (and, therefore, the 23 states and 2 territories with OSHA-approved state plans), West Virginia, and North Dakota. Most of the individual state regulations rely upon a list of hazardous substances rather than hazard assessments by the employer or manufacturer. Some form of chemical and/or product labeling is required by only 11 of 19 regulatory agencies (8 have no specific labeling requirements). Written and/or oral employee education and training are required by 17 of 19, and 14 of 19 require that the training be annual. The unique regulations vary considerably from state to state, but OSHA, as well as Maine, Oklahoma, and North Dakota, requires a Written Hazard Communication Program.

The responsibilities and rights of the various parties designated in the OSHA Standard and individual state right-to-know laws vary substantially (Table 6), reflecting the specific priorities and purposes of their legislative bodies. Some have defined responsibilities and rights in great detail, while others have chosen a more generalized, communal approach. Some have made provisions for extreme penalties, while others have chosen to levy only token fines, even after considerable compliance delays. The responsibilities summarized in Table 6 warrant a more detailed familiarity than possible in this overview. In-house, or contracted, compliance activities and programs should be based upon awareness of your specific regulatory obligations, objectives, responsibilities, and rights.

Locations of various OSHA regional offices can be found in Appendix 1, and responsible state agencies for those states with individual right-to-know laws, in Appendix 2.

APPLICABLE REGULATORY REQUIREMENTS

TABLE 1

STATES AND TERRITORIES FOLLOWING THE OSHA HAZARD COMMUNICATION STANDARD

Alaska	New York[2]
Arizona	North Carolina
California[1]	Oregon
Connecticut	Puerto Rico
Hawaii	South Carolina
Indiana	Tennessee
Iowa	Utah
Kentucky	Vermont
Maryland	Virginia
Michigan	Virgin Islands
Minnesota	Washington
Nevada	Wyoming
New Mexico	

---

1. California may be changing from the OSHA Standard to a state compliance standard in the near future.
2. New York State public schools and colleges must also comply with the State law.

TABLE 2

STATES WITH INDIVIDUAL RIGHT-TO-KNOW LAWS

Delaware	New Jersey
Florida	New York[1]
Illinois	North Dakota
Kansas	Oklahoma
Maine	Pennsylvania
Massachusetts	Rhode Island
Missouri	Texas
Montana	West Virginia
New Hampshire	Wisconsin

1. New York State schools and colleges must also comply with the OSHA Hazard Communication Standard.

TABLE 3

STATES WITH NO APPLICABLE WORKPLACE HAZARDOUS CHEMICAL REGULATIONS[1]

Alabama[2]	Louisiana
Arkansas	Mississippi
Colorado	Nebraska
District of Columbia[3]	Ohio
Georgia[4]	South Dakota

1. For public employers/institutions only. All private schools and colleges must comply with the OSHA Standard.
2. State law passed by the legislature in 1985, but never funded or implemented.
3. Follows the OSHA Standard for public and private employees, but enforcement of penalties is performed by OSHA, and then only in the private sector.
4. State law signed by the Governor on April 12, 1988, but has not been funded or implemented. Rules and regulations will not be promulgated before July 1, 1989, and then will be contingent upon funding. Applies only to *state* employees, not to all public employees, but school employees fall under this law.

TABLE 4

SPECTRUM OF HAZARDOUS CHEMICAL REGULATORY REQUIREMENTS[1]

1. Hazardous Substance List
2. Facility Inventory, Audit, or Survey
3. Data Sheets
4. Product or Chemical Research
5. Hazard Assessments of Chemicals and Products
6. Labeling
7. Written Education
8. Oral Training
9. Unique Requirements

---

1. See Table 5 for individual requirements.

Table 5

COMPARISON OF OSHA AND INDIVIDUAL STATE RIGHT-TO-KNOW REGULATORY REQUIREMENTS

Regulatory Agency (Effective Date)	Hazardous Substance List	Inventory Audit Survey	"A" Data Sheets	Product Chemical
OSHA (11/25/85)	NTP IARC "Z" List	Yes No reports	MSDS	For A & B
Delaware (1/1/85)	No	Yes Report to Fire Chief Keep on file >55 gal or 500 lb to employees when requested	MSDS	For A
Florida (1/1/85)	Yes	Yes Report to Fire Dept., Police & First Aid	MSDS	For A
Illinois (1/1/84)	Yes	Yes MSDS list to IDOL & Fire Dept.	MSDS	For A & C
Kansas (7/1/87)	No	Yes Reports: chemical list, MSDSs, emergency release with fees	MSDS	For A
Maine (1/1/80) (7/84)	Yes	Yes MSDS list	MSDS	For A
Massachusetts (11/4/83)	Yes	Not required	MSDS	For A
Missouri (12/31/86)	Yes "Z" List & TLVs	MSDSs to MDOH & Fire Dept.	MSDS	For A
Montana (4/30/85)	Yes (OSHA)	Yes Reports sent to County Clerks	MSDS	For A

"B" Hazard Assessments	"C" Labeling	Written Education	Oral Training	Unique Requirements
Written by mfr. or distr.	Identifier hazard warning by mfr.	"Training"	"Training"	Hazard Assessments Written Hazard Communication Program
Hazardous if a warning label by mfr.	Not required	Non-specific	Annual	Hazard definition = mfr. warning
		Either/Or		
No	Not required	Annual	Annual	Education & Training = MSDSs only
No	Name Hazard warning	Non-specific	Annual	Report list of MSDSs
No	Not required	Not required	Not required	Fees/report, follows SARA Title III
No	Name Hazard warning	Non-specific	Annual	Written Hazard Communication Program
No	Name NFPA Code	Either/Or		NFPA Code on labels
No	Not required	Not required	Not required	Chemicals exempt if a no-effect level exists, community RTK law
No	No	Non-specific	Annual	Nonmfr. only, mfr. = OSHA, administered by county

Table 5 (*Continued*)

Regulatory Agency (Effective Date)	Hazardous Substance List	Inventory Audit Survey	"A" Data Sheets	Product Chemical Research
New Hampshire (10/83)	Yes DOT, TVL OSHA, CA.	Yes Submit MSDSs to Fire Dept.	MSDS	For A
New Jersey (3/31/84) (12/31/85)	Yes	Yes Reports to DOH & DEP + Fire + Police Quantitative	HSFS	For A
New York (6/26/80)	RTECS (>85,000)	Yes	CDS (MSDS)	"May do"
North Dakota (7/1/85)	CERCLA	Yes	MSDS, maintain or develop	If develop A
Oklahoma 1/25/85	OSHA "Z" & "H"	Yes Per employee list of areas to Fire Dept.	MSDS, obtain or make	If develop A
Pennsylvania (10/5/85)	Yes	Yes Post list	MSDS >>reqs. (HSFS)	For A
Rhode Island (1983 & 1987)	Yes >1100	Yes Cross-referenced list, annual report to DOL, work areas to Fire Dept. on request	MSDS to Fire Dept.	For A

"B" Hazard Assessment	"C" Labeling	Written Education	Oral Training	Unique Requirements
No	No	Non-specific	Annual	MSDSs for mixtures with >2 toxic substances; + Safety & Health Law
No	Name & CAS# Five major nonhazardous ingredients	Annual	Annual	CAS# on label, hazard substance fact sheets, quantitative surveys, written & oral education
No	No	Annual	Annual	Hazard = RTECS, keep exposure records, no physical hazards, chemical data sheets
By mfr. Written evaluation procedures	Name, mfr., emergency procedures, precautions	Non-specific	Initial classroom, hands on, supervisors annual highly recommended	Written Hazard Program & Emergency Plan, training program
No	From mfr., name & CAS# Five major nonhazardous asbestos sites	Non-specific	Annual	List/employee, CAS# on label, asbestos labels, placarding, Written Hazard Program, Safety & Health Law
No	Name, hazard warning, mfr.	Non-specific	Annual	>>MSDS requirements, exposure records
No	Name, hazard warning	Non-specific	Annual employees & students, report to DOL	E & T report to DOL E & T students, list = cross-referenced

Table 5 (*Continued*)

Regulatory Agency (Effective Date)	Hazardous Substance List	Inventory Audit Survey	"A" Data Sheets	Product Chemical Research
Texas (1/1/86)	Yes (=OSHA)	Yes Report to DOL, to Fire Dept. on request	MSDS to DOH & Fire Dept. upon request	For A
West Virginia (11/25/85)	RTECS	Yes = OSHA	MSDS	For A & B
Wisconsin (1982 & 1984)	"Z" List	Yes Maintain list 30 years	MSDS	For A

"B" Hazard Assessment	"C" Labeling	Written Education	Oral Training	Unique Requirements
No	Name, hazard warning, mfr.	Non-specific	Annual employees & students, report to DOH	E & T report to DOH E & T students
= OSHA	= OSHA	= OSHA	= OSHA	Applies only to public worksites; creates new state division, review commission & advisory board
No	No	Either/Or		Notify parent of minor employee; covers infectious agents, pesticides, and chemicals

TABLE 6

SUMMARY OF OSHA AND INDIVIDUAL STATE RIGHT-TO-KNOW RESPONSIBILITIES

Regulatory Agency	Agency Responsibilities	Employers Affected	Employer Responsibilities
OSHA (+ 26 States & 2 Territories)	Develop hazard assessment criteria. Identify basic hazardous chemicals. Inspect worksites.	1985-Chemical manufacturers. 1988-All private employers and public employers in states with OSHA approved plans.	Written hazard communication program. Written hazard assessment criteria. MSDSs on file. Employee education & training. Container labeling.
Delaware	Develop posters, pamphlets and training materials. Inspect worksites. Verify trade secrets. Certify nonmanufacturers for compliance with the OSHA Standard.	All employers doing business in the state. (This law was designed to complement the OSHA Standard.)	Develop a Workplace Chemical List of hazardous chemicals >55 gals or 500 lbs annually. Provide MSDSs & employee training. Post the Employee Rights notice. Identify...
Florida	Establish toxic substance list, revise annually. Disseminate literature regarding toxic substances. Assist employers.	Employers with 5 or more employees except for certain agricultural & pesticide employers.	Post employee rights notice. Obtain MSDSs & provide to employees upon request. Train employees each year. Notify Fire Dept. regarding locations of toxic substances.
Illinois	Publish toxic substance list, employer poster, duties & rights of employers & employees, list of MSDSs. Investigate complaints.	Employers with full-time or a total of 20 employees, with some exceptions.	Post a Right-To-Know sign. Obtain an MSDS for each toxic substance. Submit a list of MSDSs to DOL. Label all toxic substances with chemical name & hazard warning. Notify Fire Dept. about toxic substances.

Employee Rights	Community Rights	Penalties
Access to hazard data & information. MSDSs upon request. Hazardous substance list. Training by employer.	None under OSHA Standard, combines with SARA Title III from EPA to provide Community Rights.	$1000/violation & $500/day. $10,000 for willful violations.
Informed of exposures. Access to MSDSs. Receive training/year. Receive personal protective equipment. Access to Workplace Chemical List. Cannot be penalized for exercising rights.	Fire Chiefs receive MSDSs. Workplace Chemical Lists & identity of company responsible persons. Fire Chiefs can inspect worksites.	$500/violation, civil penalty.
Access to list of toxic substances. MSDSs & information from the state. Annual training. Refuse to work under specified circumstances.	Fire Dept. informed of location and types of toxic substances.	$1000 for each violation, civil penalty.
Access to MSDSs within 10 days. Annual training. Refuse to work with a toxic substance without an MSDS.	Fire Dept. notified about toxic substances.	$1000 for each violation & $10,000 for repeat violations.

Table 6 (*Continued*)

Regulatory Agency	Agency Responsibilities	Employers Affected	Employer Responsibilities
Kansas	Supplements SARA Title III Community Right-To-Know Act. Establish local planning districts. Develop regulations & set fees. Assess fines & penalties.	All employers with specific "extremely hazardous substances."	Provide notifications, list of chemicals present, MSDSs & annual reports to state, including Tier I & Tier II inventory reports & toxic waste emission inventories.
Maine	Publish annual list of hazardous substances. Assist employer in getting MSDSs. Administer the training assistance fund. Inspect employers.	All employers with hazardous chemicals.	Inventory & file annual hazardous chemical list. Develop a Written Hazard Communication Program. Label hazardous chemical containers. Conduct annual refresher training for employees. Provide MSDSs to DOL. Pay annual fee.
Massachusetts	Develop hazardous substance list & update annually. Distribute health hazard information. Enforce MSDS procedures & retain MSDSs from employers. Investigate employee complaints. Establish community data coordinators.	All employers with chemicals, only a few exceptions.	Post employee notice. Label containers of hazardous substances with chemical name & NFPA Codes. File MSDSs with DEQE & municipal coordinator. Provide annual employee training.
Missouri	Develop toxic substance list. Receive employer MSDSs & provide to requesters, including emergency personnel. Review trade secret claims.	Any employer with 1 kg carcinogen, 55 gal liquid, 500 lbs solid, 200 cu ft gas.	Provide MSDSs for toxic substances to DNR & Fire Dept., update annually. Permit on-site inspection by Fire Dept. Provide Fire Dept. 2 names for contact.

Employee Rights	Community Rights	Penalties
Community rights as citizens. No other employee rights.	Access to inventories, chemical lists, and emission reports.	$10,000 for each violation & $10,000 to $75,000/day of violation, civil. Criminal = $50,000 or 5 years in prison.
Examine chemical list, MSDSs & hazardous chemical exposure records. Receive annual training.	Fire Chiefs can request hazardous chemical lists and MSDSs.	$500–1000 for each violation.
Receive annual training. Review MSDSs within 4 days of request. If delayed, or MSDS is incomplete, can refuse to work with the substance.	MSDSs retained by community coordinator. Residents can request MSDSs and investigation of hazardous chemical usage.	$250 for each day violated, civil. $500 for willful violations and/or 30 days imprisoned. $1000/day and/or 90 days for repeat violations.
None	Fire Dept. receives MSDSs and conducts on-site inspections. Anyone can request MSDS from DOH.	Up to $5000 for intentional violations.

Table 6 (*Continued*)

Regulatory Agency	Agency Responsibilities	Employers Affected	Employer Responsibilities
Montana	DOLI to develop education and training program as well as informational posters & brochures. Investigate employee complaints. Fire Chief to inspect community information annually & perform on-site inspections. County Clerk to compile MSDS index for public reference.	All employers with hazardous chemicals.	Compile annual Workplace Chemical List. Post employee rights notice. Provide annual employee education program. Submit MSDSs, Workplace List & company personnel information to County Clerk. Do not remove or deface labels.
New Hampshire	DOL develop toxics list, file MSDSs & investigate employee complaints.	All employers in state.	Post warning notice of toxic substances & notice of MSDS availability. Provide employee education & training. Tell employees of their rights. Keep MSDS file. Provide MSDSs & identify chemical locations to Fire Dept. Obtain new hazard information.
New Jersey	DOH to develop workplace survey, hazard substance list & Hazardous Substance Fact Sheets for employers. DEP to develop environmental list & survey. DOL to investigate discrimination & assess employer fees. Right-To-Know Advisory Council chosen by Governor.	SIC Codes 20–39, 46–49, 51, 75, 76, 80, 82, & 84 (includes most employers in the state).	Conduct annual workplace & environmental surveys & send to state and local agencies. Keep Central Information File. Conduct annual employee written & oral education & training. Post notices from DOH & label containers of hazardous, nonhazardous & "contents unknown" substances.

Employee Rights	Community Rights	Penalties
Access to MSDSs and Workplace List. Annual training. Protective equipment. Protection from recriminations for exercising rights.	Access to MSDSs and Workplace Lists with County Clerk. Fire Chief to perform on-site inspections.	Misdemeanor for each violation & each day of violation.
MSDS access in 72 hrs. and education & training. Refuse to work if MSDS not provided in 72 hrs.	MSDSs and chemical location filed with Fire Dept.	$2500 for each violation or each day of violation.
Access to workplace & environmental surveys. Hazardous Substance Fact Sheets & label data. Annual written & oral education & training. Refuse to work if data not provided within 5 working days.	Copies of workplace & environmental surveys & Hazardous Substance Fact Sheets from state & local agencies. Bring a civil action against an employer.	$2500 for each violation & $1000 for each day violation continues.

Table 6 (*Continued*)

Regulatory Agency	Agency Responsibilities	Employers Affected	Employer Responsibilities
New York	DOH to develop kit to help employers comply (includes signs & informational leaflets). Develop Chemical Fact Sheets (CFSs). Investigate complaints.	All employers in the state.	Post signs & provide DOH leaflets to employees. Keep employee exposure records for 40 yrs. Conduct annual employee training. Obtain MSDSs from mfr. & maintain file of data.
North Dakota	Workmen's Compensation Bureau to develop employer guidelines, notices & inspect workplaces for violations.	All employers that use hazardous substances—on CERCLA list.	Conduct inventory for hazardous substances. Post employee notices. Obtain MSDSs & properly label containers. Develop emergency plans & conduct employee & supervisor training. Establish written hazard evaluation procedures. Monitor work areas to assure they are safe & healthful.
Oklahoma	DOL to develop rules. Fire Chief files noncompliance complaint. Establish Hazard Communication Committee to study emergency and hazard problems.	All private & public, including mfrs.	Inventory, develop a Chemical Information List (CIL) for facility & each employee, & update yearly. Maintain MSDS file & container labels. Provide annual employee education & training. Label sources of asbestos.

Employee Rights	Community Rights	Penalties
DOH leaflets and CFSs. Annual training & access to exposure records. Refuse to work if requested data for a toxic substance not provided in 72 hrs.	Access to toxic substance data & information.	Noncompliance $10,000 fine. Willful violation = $500–1000 fine & ≤90 days in jail.
Access to MSDSs and safe & healthful work area. Classroom and "hands-on" training. Container labels. Access to chemical inventory.	None.	Penalties pursuant to NDCC 65-03-02.
Access to CIL & MSDSs within 15 days. Annual education & training. Labels for 5 most predominant substances. Refuse to work when information not provided. Must report exposures & work safely as trained.	None.	Pursuant to Title 40, Chapter 10 of Oklahoma OHSSA.

Table 6 (*Continued*)

Regulatory Agency	Agency Responsibilities	Employers Affected	Employer Responsibilities
Pennsylvania	DOLI to develop Outreach Program for employers, employees & public. Can include leaflets, notices & public announcements. Investigate complaints from employees, citizens & public agencies. Develop list of hazardous substances. Design workplace & environmental forms.	All employers in the state, public & private.	Conduct workplace survey of hazardous substances & post. Conduct environmental survey upon request from DOLI. Compile MSDSs & maintain labels for top 5 components. Provide annual employee training. Maintain employee exposure records. Provide fire, police & emergency agencies with hazardous substance list, environmental survey & MSDSs upon request.
Rhode Island	DOL to establish Commission on Hazardous Substances in the Workplace, Designated Substances List, & collect $35 annual fee from employers. DOH to assist employers, employees, & public safety personnel with training programs. Provide available MSDSs to public. DOL to inspect for compliance.	Any employer that uses toxic or hazardous substances.	Develop Chemical Identification List (CIL) & obtain MSDSs. Label containers, post signs, or placards. Revise CIL every year & keep 30 years. Give list of work areas with designated substances & MSDSs to fire dept. Provide full list of substances involved in an emergency within 48 hours. Annual employee training. Provide CIL & MSDSs to subcontractors.

Employee Rights	Community Rights	Penalties
Access to hazardous substance list, MSDSs & exposure records. Annual training & state leaflets and notices.	DOLI Outreach Program & employer environmental hazard survey. MSDSs & workplace surveys.	$500–10,000 for each violation. $5,000/day that the violation continues.
Access to CIL & MSDSs within 3 days. Refuse to work if information not provided. Annual training.	Access to Designated Substances List and any available MSDS.	$5,000/day of violation. Imprisonment for willful violations.

Table 6 (*Continued*)

Regulatory Agency	Agency Responsibilities	Employers Affected	Employer Responsibilities
Texas	DOH to develop outreach program including training program, employee rights notices, & informational leaflets. Investigate complaints.	SIC Codes 20–39, 46–49, 51, 75, 76, 80, 82 & 84.	Compile Workplace Chemical List yearly for materials in excess of 55 gals or 500 lbs & send to DOH. Obtain MSDSs from mfr. and provide to DOH & Fire Chief. Provide Fire Chief with list of company emergency personnel and workplace chemical list. Post employee rights notice. Maintain container labels. Provide annual employee training, notify DOH when completed.
West Virginia	DOL to develop rules, education program, employer and employee materials reporting procedures, inspect worksites, create temporary standards, publish inspection findings.	All *public* employers only.	Furnish workplace free from life-threatening or serious hazards. Compile list of toxic substances. Comply with OSHA Standards. Receive training from DOL.
Wisconsin	DILHR to develop brochure and employee rights notice, maintain records for out-of-business employers. Investigate complaints.	All employers, including agricultural.	Compile toxic substance list & maintain for 30 yrs. if containers each 1 kg or use >10 kg/year. Obtain MSDSs & infectious agent data. Provide employers requested information. Provide employee training. Notify parent of minor employee rights.

Employee Rights	Community Rights	Penalties
Access to Workplace Chemical List & MSDSs. Annual training and appropriate personal protective equipment. Exercise rights without discrimination by employer.	Workplace Chemical List & MSDSs filed with Fire Dept. Fire Chief to conduct on-site inspections.	$500/violation or $5,000 for each willful violation. $25,000 if proximately the cause of an injury.
Access to toxic substance list and information. Training by DOL. Exercise rights without employer discrimination.	None.	None; citations only.
Access to toxic substances list and information. Access to infectious agent and pesticide data. Training. Exercise rights without employer discrimination.	None.	$1000/violation or $10,000 for each willful violation.

HOW TO COMPLY

STEP 1

REGULATORY REVIEW, COMPLIANCE ASSIGNMENTS

Obtain a copy of the regulations that apply to your school or college from one of the following sources:

1. The OSHA Hazard Communication Standard, available from the nearest OSHA office (see Appendix 1).

2. The November 25, 1985, and the August 24, 1987, *Federal Register.*

3. The Code of Federal Regulations at 1910.1200.

4. The appropriate state right-to-know regulations from the responsible state agency (see Appendix 2).

Assign the responsibility for compliance within your school or college to one person. Be aware that the total task of program definition, development, and implementation will require various experts from within or outside your organization (e.g., policy development, data acquisition, hazard assessment, training).

STEP 2

NEEDS ANALYSIS, CHEMICAL INVENTORY, POLICY AUDIT

Evaluate your current receiving, production, and employee communication procedures in light of the applicable OSHA or state requirements. Identify all chemicals and products in your workplace by surveying all work areas, warehouses, storage sites, and maintenance areas. You must compile lists of purchased materials and supplier addresses and compare internal policies to OSHA or state requirements. Deficiencies and inadequacies in your present policies indicate areas for new initiatives to achieve compliance. This activity provides the basis for developing a focused and efficient plan to achieve full compliance in a cost-effective and timely manner.

STEP 3

POLICY DEVELOPMENT

Establish written facility guidelines and principles that will provide the foundation for all subsequent, specific compliance activities. Deficiencies in school or college policies often include:

1. Lack of standardized nomenclature for purchased materials.

2. Inappropriate mechanisms and procedures for obtaining and utilizing new purchased chemicals or products.

3. Unnecessary, unwarranted, and aged chemical and product inventories in science, art, industrial art, custodial, maintenance, and administration chemical storage areas.

4. Uncontrolled chemical or product labeling (especially materials already in inventory prior to implementation of the applicable federal or state regulations).

5. Insufficient and/or outdated chemical and product data.

6. Insufficient or nonexistent hazard assessment criteria.

7. Inappropriate protective equipment standards.

8. Inadequate and/or inappropriate employee training procedures.

9. Absence of administrative and functional hazardous chemical and product responsibility assignments.

Policies 1, 2, and 3 above are practical suggestions for establishing and maintaining your hazard communication program. Items 4 through 9 are required by the OSHA Standard and most individual state right-to-know regulations as well. Proper correction of these nine common deficiencies will obviously require implementation of new policies and procedures in most schools and colleges, but early establishment of these new functions will facilitate improvements in your hazardous chemical safety and health program and greatly expedite completion of subsequent phases of your compliance efforts.

STEP 4

HAZARD COMMUNICATION PROGRAM SUMMARY

The OSHA, Maine, Oklahoma, and North Dakota regulations require each employer to develop and implement a Written Hazard Communication Program that describes how criteria for material safety data sheets, labels, and other forms of warning and employee information and training will be met. Many schools and colleges in other states should also consider developing a similar summary, even though not required by law, since the criteria and objectives will facilitate development of the overall program and assure effective communication to various levels of their administration.

This summary must also include a list of your hazardous chemicals, a description of methods you will use to inform employees of the hazards associated with nonroutine tasks (e.g., equipment maintenance/cleanup), and procedures used to inform any outside contractor-employer of hazardous chemicals his or her employees may encounter at your workplace. (A Written Hazard Communication Program that can be easily supplemented and/or customized by your school or college staff is available as part of this series. See *Series Description.*)

STEP 5

DATA ACQUISITION AND COMPILATION

This activity not only is the most time-consuming phase in your compliance program, but also represents the area of greatest importance. The OSHA Standard, and essentially every state right-to-know law, requires employers to convey hazardous chemical and product information to their employees, as well as to some community organizations in several states, through a variety of formats. These include data sheets, labels, education and training programs, and lists or reports. Poor hazardous chemical and product information and data will greatly compromise the quality and integrity of your safety, health, and compliance programs.

Promulgation of the OSHA Standard, and many of the state right-to-know regulations, essentially made all existing material safety data sheets (MSDSs) obsolete (see Appendix 3E). Consequently, information provided by your chemical and product suppliers may be inadequate for regulatory compliance. Remember, chemical manufacturers, importers, and distributors must comply with the OSHA Standard and, therefore, the MSDS informational and content requirements of the federal regulations. On the other hand, your school or college may be required to comply with a state regulation that may differ in some of the data details from the OSHA Standard, or you may choose to include additional information, such as on proper disposal, that is not specifically required by OSHA. Your sources for chemical information may include:

1. Your chemical and product suppliers.

2. Your state Departments of Health, Labor, or Environment.

3. Professional publications found in your science department or your school or college library.

4. Supplemental research conducted by qualified staff or consultants familiar with chemical hazard data and assessments.

Suggested survey letters, questionnaires, and data formats are included in Appendix 3.

To comply with the OSHA Standard, or 17 of 19 individual state right-to-know laws (Table 5), you must obtain an MSDS from your supplier for each purchased chemical or product in your inventory (Step 2 above), and you must develop an MSDS for every chemical mixture or formulation that is produced by any department in your school or college. These MSDSs must be kept on file for employee use and OSHA or state inspection. New information must be added to an MSDS within three months from the date that new information was obtained. The adequacy of information in your MSDSs will greatly influence the quality and adequacy of your hazard assessments, training program, and labels. As new materials enter your workplace, MSDSs must be acquired or developed, and employees trained *before the new materials are introduced into the workplace.*

STEP 6

HAZARD ASSESSMENTS

This activity requires the greatest level of technical expertise. Many chemical manufacturers and distributors do not, in fact, have adequate professional staff to properly perform this most critical responsibility. Consequently, even though non-manufacturers under the OSHA Standard* and all employers under the individual state right-to-know laws are not *required* to perform hazard assessments, you should be aware of the possibility of inadequate hazard assessment information from manufacturers or distributors so that faulty assessments can be and are identified.

Public schools and colleges in states with individual right-to-know laws (Table 2), or in states with no applicable hazardous chemical regulations (Table 3), are not required to perform hazard assessments. States with individual right-to-know laws generally provide a list of hazardous chemicals that have been so designated by the responsible state agency. Purchased products, however, must be researched to identify which, if any, of the designated hazardous chemicals are components in the products.

In addition, we highly recommend that every public and private school and college become sufficiently aware of appropriate hazard assessment criteria and procedures that they can and will identify liabilities associated with using faulty or inadequate hazard assessment information from suppliers and distributors. In fact, we also recommend that

---

*This includes all private schools and colleges and those public schools and colleges that reside within one of the states or territories with an OSHA-approved state plan, listed in Table 1.

you obtain, review, and maintain on file the hazard assessment criteria for each of your manufacturers or suppliers.

As a responsible administrator, you should not assume that hazard assessments by chemical manufacturers or distributors are adequate and correct, but should verify that this most critical procedure meets school or college standards and expectations. Many school and college administrators initially approach hazardous chemical compliance policies and procedures from the "what is the least that I can get by with" attitude until an employee or student is injured in a chemical accident. Suddenly, the priority, dollars, and staff time to implement appropriate procedures all become available. Over 1500 hazardous chemical accidents were reported in schools and colleges in the past year—*don't let your school or college become part of this statistic!* Focus upon proper management of this potentially serious subject by implementing responsible policies and procedures rather than concentrating upon the minimum regulatory requirements.

Assessments for schools and colleges complying with the OSHA Standard must be based upon criteria promulgated in the federal regulation, stated school or college policies, and accepted scientific principles. Information provided by manufacturers or distributors for purchased chemicals and products must encompass both health (i.e., acute and chronic) and physical (i.e., fire, reactivity, and explosivity) hazards. Your list of chemicals and products deemed hazardous must be maintained on file (see Step 7 below) and updated whenever new materials become classified as hazardous. All hazardous materials must be properly labeled in accordance with the OSHA Standard (see Step 8 below), and employees "potentially" exposed to hazardous chemicals must be trained with regard to the hazards of those chemicals or products (see

Step 9 below). If the hazard assessments are properly performed, they can be readily integrated with MSDS review procedures, labeling information, and employee education and training.

Numerous hazard assessment criteria have been published and can be used in your chemical and product evaluations. The criteria found in Appendix 4 are usable by schools and colleges that must comply with either the OSHA Standard or individual state right-to-know laws.

STEP 7

DATA FILE MAINTENANCE

Your hazard communication data files must fulfill two over-lapping responsibilities, regardless of whether or not you must comply with the OSHA Standard or an individual state right-to-know law:

1. Regulatory compliance

2. "Good faith" documentation

The first function covers information that must be available to employees (items 2, 3, 4, and 6 in the list below). Documents you maintain for the second objective may be kept as confidential. You should be certain that your files contain at least the following documents:

1. Supplier correspondence

2. Chemical and product data sheets (e.g., MSDSs)

3. List of hazardous chemicals

4. Written Hazard Communication Program Summary (for those schools and colleges that must comply with the OSHA Standard, Maine, Oklahoma, and North Dakota State Right-To-Know laws, or choose to use this document voluntarily)

5. Criteria for hazard assessments, MSDSs, and labels

6. Training resources and records

These files should be continuously maintained to assure adequate, supportive documentation for OSHA or state agency inspections, insurance information, employee inquiries, public relations issues, and management awareness. Some regulations stipulate the duration that information must be retained in this file, but the retention period varies from agency to agency.

Since employees and regulatory inspectors must have access to your information, separate files should be maintained in every school or campus location that has an individual mailing address to avoid citations and penalties.

STEP 8

LABEL GENERATION

The OSHA Standard requires that all containers of hazardous materials be properly labeled, but 8 of 19 states with individual right-to-know laws do not include a labeling requirement. In order to comply with the OSHA Standard, label information for purchased chemicals and products must include:

1. Identity of the hazardous chemicals,

2. Appropriate hazard warnings, and

3. Name and address of the manufacturer or distributor.

Hazard warnings may be in the form of words, pictures, or symbols that convey the chemical hazard(s). Most of the remaining 11 of 19 states with individual right-to-know laws require similar label information, but several of these states have additional or different requirements (e.g., Chemical Abstract Service Registry Numbers).

The OSHA Standard requires that the manufacturer or distributor insure that this labeling requirement is fulfilled, but each manufacturer or distributor is free to develop a unique format for providing the required hazard information. Consequently, every source of chemical or product will provide a different labeling system. This will greatly complicate hazard communication to your employees, since they will need to understand many different, sometimes coded, labeling systems.

Alternatively, your school or college may choose to implement an internal labeling program for all purchased chemicals and products as they are received. This approach not only will increase employee awareness of hazardous chemical information, but can also complement your education and training program by providing a single label standard that can be much more easily incorporated into your written and/or oral training program. A single label system will also serve as a continuous training tool for new or transferred employees.

STEP 9

EMPLOYEE TRAINING

Most of the states with individual right-to-know laws require annual education and training of employees with "potential exposure" (e.g., accidental or possible). The OSHA Standard does not stipulate the frequency of training, but does indicate that employees must be trained "whenever a new hazard is introduced into their work area." Only New Jersey and New York states specifically require that both written and oral training be provided, but our direct experience, as well as historic experience of educators, supports the concept that employees will assimilate more information in a shorter time when training is presented in both written *and* oral formats.

Your employee education program should provide information regarding:

1. The OSHA Standard or applicable state regulations,

2. Areas where hazardous chemicals are present,

3. The location and availability of your Written Hazard Communication Program Summary, if required or utilized,

4. MSDSs or other data sheets, and

5. Your list of hazardous chemicals.

In addition, employee training should include the detection of hazardous chemicals, physical and health hazards of your workplace chemicals and products, and the proper use of protective measures and equipment, as well as how employees can obtain and use appropriate hazard information. (The outlines for an initial Employee Training Manual in Appendix 5 and an initial Employee Seminar in Appendix 6 are presented for those schools and colleges that prefer to develop their own capabilities. Alternatively, your school district or college may choose to use all or part of the Comprehensive Hazard Communication and Right-To-Know Compliance Program summarized in the Series Description at the back of this book.)

STEP 10

PROGRAM MAINTENANCE

Your school or college must both develop a program that fulfills all of the state or federal regulatory requirements (and whatever internal standards you may elect to establish) and implement procedures that will assure continuous adherence to these requirements and standards. Your maintenance program will become much more "automatic" if you have carefully planned your policies and procedures from the beginning. For example, adjustments in your chemical purchasing procedures, within your institution or individual departments, not only will provide required data sheets and proper labeling in an ongoing manner, but also can provide hazardous chemical and product inventory control, safer chemical storage, and proper chemical disposal. Maintenance of proper labels is a particular responsibility that must be carefully planned, especially in those states with unique labeling requirements that will not be fulfilled by chemical manufacturers or distributors who must comply with the OSHA Standard. Hazard communication responsibilities that will need regular or intermittent maintenance include the following:

1. Policy, procedure, and regulatory review (annual)

2. Data sheet acquisition, review, and updating

3. Data assimilation and communication procedures

4. Data incorporation into employee training

5. Label review and/or maintenance

6. Hazardous substance list updating

7. Chemical and product inventory evaluation

8. Chemical storage practices

9. Chemical disposal frequency and procedures (especially for deteriorated containers, aged chemicals or products, and discontinued materials)

10. Emergency response procedures and capabilities

Items 1 to 6 address specific regulatory requirements, whereas 7 to 10 involve procedures that many forward-thinking school and college administrators have implemented to help them more effectively control chemical hazards and, thereby, substantially reduce their risks for chemical accidents and subsequent liability lawsuits while simultaneously improving their employee and public relations.

APPENDIXES

APPENDIX 1

REGIONAL OCCUPATIONAL SAFETY AND HEALTH ADMINISTRATION OFFICES

REGION I
(CT, MA, ME, NH, RI, VT)

6-18 North Street
1 Dock Square Building
4th Floor
Boston, Massachusetts 02109
(617) 565-1145

REGION II
(NY, NJ, PR, VI)

201 Varick Street
Room 670
New York, New York 10014
(212) 337-2325

REGION III
(DC, DE, MD, PA, VA, WV)

Gateway Building, Suite 2100
3535 Market Street
Philadelphia, Pennsylvania 19104
(215) 596-1201

REGION IV
(AL, FL, GA, KY, MS, NC, SC, TN)

1375 Peachtree Street, N.E.
Suite 587
Atlanta, Georgia 30367
(404) 347-3573

REGION V
(IL, IN, MI, MN, OH, WI)

230 South Dearborn Street
32nd Floor, Room 3244
Chicago, Illinois 60604
(312) 353-2220

REGION VI
(AR, LA, NM, OK, TX)

525 Griffin Square Building
Room 602
Dallas, Texas 75202
(214) 767-4731

REGION VII
(IA, KS, MO, NE)

911 Walnut Street
Room 406
Kansas City, Missouri 64106
(816) 426-5861

REGION VIII
(CO, MT, ND, SD, UT, WY)

Federal Building, Room 1576
1961 Stout Street
Denver, Colorado 80294
(303) 844-3061

REGION IX
(AZ, CA, HI, NV, +3 Terrs.)

71 Stevenson Street
Room 415
San Francisco, California 94105
(415) 995-5672

REGION X
(AK, ID, OR, WA)

Federal Office Building
Room 6003
909 First Avenue
Seattle, Washington 98174
(206) 442-5930

APPENDIX 2

RESPONSIBLE STATE AGENCIES FOR STATES WITH INDIVIDUAL RIGHT-TO-KNOW LAWS

DELAWARE

Bureau of Environmental Health
Division of Public Health
Department of Health & Social
Services
Jesse Cooper Building
P.O. Box 637
Dover, Delaware 19901
(302) 736-3839

FLORIDA

Bureau of Industrial Safety &
Health
Toxic Substances Information
Center
2551 Executive Center
Circle West, Lafayette Building
Tallahassee, Florida 32301
(904) 488-9660/(800) 367-4378

ILLINOIS

Toxic Substance Division
Illinois Department of Labor
100 North First Street
5th Floor North
Springfield, Illinois 62706
(217) 782-4102

KANSAS

Department of Health and Environment
Building 728 Forbes Field
6700 SW Topeka Street
Topeka, Kansas 66620
(913) 296-1690

MAINE

Bureau of Labor
Industrial Safety Division
Station 82
State Office Building
Augusta, Maine 04333
(207) 289-2591

MASSACHUSETTS

Right To Know Office
Department of Labor & Industry
100 Cambridge Street
Room 1107
Boston, Massachusetts 02202
(617) 727-5816

MISSOURI

Department of Health
Bureau of Environmental
Epidemiology
Community Right To Know
Program
P.O. Box 570
Jefferson City, Missouri 65102
(314) 751-6400

MONTANA

Department of Labor & Industry
Division of Occupational
Safety and Health
Helena, Montana 59601
(406) 444-6401

NEW HAMPSHIRE

Inspection Division
Department of Labor
19 Pillsbury Street
Concord, New Hampshire 03301
(603) 271-3170

NEW JERSEY

Department of Health
Right To Know Project
CN 368
Trenton, New Jersey 08625
(609) 984-2202

NEW YORK

Department of Health
Division of Environmental Health
Bureau of Toxic Substance Assessment
Empire State Plaza
Corning Tower
Albany, New York 12237
(518) 473-7238

NORTH DAKOTA

Workmen's Compensation
Bureau
Russel Building, Highway 83 No.
4007 North State Street
Bismark, North Dakota 58501
(701) 224-2700

OKLAHOMA

Occupational Hazards Division
Department of Labor
1315 Broadway Place
Oklahoma City, Oklahoma 73103
(405) 235-0530

PENNSYLVANIA

Right To Know Office
Labor and Industry Building
Room 1404
Harrisburg, Pennsylvania 17120
(717) 783-2071

RHODE ISLAND

Department of Labor
Division of Occupational Safety
Right To Know Office
220 Elmwood Avenue
Providence, Rhode Island 02907
(401) 277-2756

WEST VIRGINIA

Department of Labor
Safety and Boiler Division
Building 3, Room 319
1800 Washington Street East
Charleston, West Virginia 25305
(304) 348-7890

TEXAS

Department of Health
Occupational Safety and Health
Program
1100 West 49th Street
Austin, Texas 78756
(512) 458-7254

WISCONSIN

Division of Safety & Buildings
Department of Industry, Labor
and Human Relations
P.O. Box 7969
Madison, Wisconsin 53707
(608) 226-2780

APPENDIX 3

DATA ACQUISITION FROM SUPPLIERS

Information for hazardous chemicals or products in your school or college may be obtained through:

1. Your responsible state agency (see Appendix 2),

2. Your chemical and product suppliers, or

3. Supplemental research performed by, or for, your school or college.

Materials in this Appendix are presented as a packet that can be submitted to your suppliers to assure that you receive required information for your internal hazard communication program.

The first three documents in this Appendix each serve a distinct purpose. The *Supplier Survey Letter* can be used to obtain hazardous chemical or product information from your supplier. *Hazard Communication Data Requirements* summarizes OSHA data requirements for MSDSs provided by your supplier, or developed by your school or college. The data requirements for the individual state right-to-know laws vary considerably, but this basic set of OSHA requirements could serve as a good "internal" school or college standard if your state requirements are less stringent. Responses to the *Supplemental Supplier Questionnaire* will provide important hazard information that is often omitted from MSDSs, but that will greatly strengthen your overall hazard communication program. When your suppliers return MSDSs in response to your requests, the two attachments to the letter in this pack-

APPENDIX 3B

HAZARD COMMUNICATION DATA REQUIREMENTS

1. **CHEMICAL IDENTITY:**

   Chemical, Common and Trade Names; CAS No.; Mixture or Single Material

2. **PHYSICAL/ CHEMICAL PROPERTIES:**

   Water Solubility, Vapor Pressure, Flash point, Specific Gravity, Boiling Point, Volatility, Appearance, and Color

3. **PHYSICAL HAZADS:**

   Fire, Explosivity, Reactivity

4. **HEALTH HAZARDS:**

   Acute and Chronic Effects, Animal and Human Test Results, Symptoms of Exposure, Medical Conditions Aggravated by, Registry of Toxic Effects of Chemical Substances (RTECS) Data Summation, Listed by OSHA/NTP/IARC

5. **ROUTES OF ENTRY:**

   OSHA and ACGIH Threshold Limit Values (TLVs), Exposure Mechanisms

et can be used to verify that the MSDSs fulfill OSHA or applicable state right-to-know requirements.

The *Data Base Format* in this Appendix will be useful primarily to those schools and colleges that plan to computerize their hazardous chemical or product information. This particular format includes data that fulfill OSHA and all state right-to-know data requirements. The *Material Safety Data Sheets* section and the *Sample MSDS Format* illustrate the content and scope of information that should be included in MSDSs sent by your suppliers.

APPENDIX 3A

SAMPLE SUPPLIER SURVEY LETTER

(This letter should be sent on your letterhead to all suppliers of chemicals and products for every department in your school or college.)

Dear _____ :

   (*Name of your school or college*) is currently implementing procedures that will assure our full compliance with either our state right-to-know (RTK) law or the OSHA Hazard Communication Standard. As you are probably aware, these regulations require us to make data and assessments available to our employees. In the past, we understand that many organizations made material safety data sheets (MSDSs) available for this purpose. However, detailed data and assessment requirements in federal and many state regulations encompass information not previously required in MSDSs (e.g., CAS Registry Numbers, chronic health data summaries, medical conditions aggravated by exposure, etc.). In fact, we understand that OSHA officially discontinued use of their two-page MSDS, or OSHA Form-20, several years ago because of these more extensive data requirements.

   The attached table (*use Appendix 3B*) summarizes the composite information required by federal and state hazard communication regulations. In addition, however, we must also comply with a variety of other local, state, and federal regulations. Consequently, we would appreciate your assistance in providing us with as much technical and regulatory information as possible. To aid you with our request, we have attached a Supplemental Supplier Questionnaire (*use Appendix 3C*) that will provide information we currently anticipate will be essential to our hazard communication program. To assure our full compliance with

---

these diverse regulations, we request that you send t[...] each material purchased from you by (*name of your* [...] (Please indicate "N/A," Not Applicable, or "D/U," D[...] spaces, if necessary, rather than leaving blanks.)

   If you have any questions regarding this mat[...] policies/procedures, please contact (*name of respor* [...] (*telephone number*). Your completed forms should [...] *your school or college*) and be mailed to :

(*Name and Title*)
(*Department, School/College*)
(*Street Address*)
(*City, State, Zip Code*)
(*Telephone*)

   Please notify (*name of responsible individual*) [...] completed form will not be available to us within [...]

   Your expeditious assistance in this matter is ap[...]

Very truly yours,

(*Name*)
(*Title*)

Enclosures: Hazard Communications Data Re[...]
                Supplemental Supplier Questionn[...]
cc:

6. **FIRST AID PROCEDURES:**   Emergency Contact Person and Telephone No., Recommended Treatment

7. **HANDLING PRECAUTIONS:**   Hygienic Practices, Protective Equipment, Appropriate Fire Extinguisher(s), Work Practices, Engineering Controls (i.e., Ventilation, etc.), Detection Methods

8. **ENVIRONMENTAL HAZARDS:**   Air/Water/Soil, Biodegradability, Spill/Leak Cleanup Procedures, Disposal Procedures, Container Hazard(s), Priority Pollutant

9. **LABEL:**   Chemical Identity, Hazard Warnings, Name and Address of Supplier/Distributor

10. **DATE OF LAST CHANGE:**   Revised Data Provided with Next Shipment

11. **DISTRIBUTOR/ PREPARER:**   Name, Address, and Telephone No.

APPENDIX 3C
SUPPLEMENTAL SUPPLIER QUESTIONNAIRE

(*Purchased Material Identity*)

	No	Yes	Other
1. Is this material a combination of ingredients (i.e., a mixture)?	____	____	____
2. If this material is a mixture, does it contain any hazardous components above 0.1%? Please list:	____	____	____

_____

_____

3. Do you claim a trade secret for the Specific Chemical Identity of this material, or any components?	____	____	____
4. Has your hazard assessment for this material considered both physical (fire, explosion, and reactivity) and health risks (acute *and* chronic)?	____	____	____
5. Is this material recognized as hazardous by you, OSHA, NTP, IARC, or any other government agency or trade? Please explain:_____	____	____	____

_____

_____

	No	Yes	Other

6. Are there any "Foresee-
   able Emergencies" (as
   defined by the OSHA
   Standard) that can in-
   crease, change, or create
   hazardous circumstances
   for this material? Please
   explain:_____

   _____

   _____

7. Do you recommend any
   special precautions or handling procedures for this
   material? Please explain:

   _____

   _____

8. Do you use "hazard warnings" on your label for this
   material? Please describe:

   _____

   _____

9. Are there medical conditions that may be ag-
   gravated by exposure to
   this material? Please list:

   _____

   _____

10. Have either your company
    or your customers ever
    recorded employee or con-
    sumer reactions? Please
    list:_____

    _____

    _____

	No	Yes	Other
11. What are the signs and symptoms of exposure to this material? Please list:	___	___	___
_____			
_____			
12. Does this material have an odor detection limit (in ppm or % in air)? Value:	___	___	___
_____			
13. Are there other "methods and observations that may be used to detect the presence or release of (this material)"? Please list:	___	___	___
_____			
_____			
14. Is this material bio-degradable? Supportive evidence:_____	___	___	___
_____			
_____			
15. Does this material present environmental risks (air, water, or soil)? Please explain:_____	___	___	___
_____			
_____			
16. Do you have an MSDS that fulfills data requirements of the OSHA Standard? Please attach.	___	___	___

	No	Yes	Other
17. Do you have an individual or department responsible for your MSDSs? Name/Title:_____ Telephone:_____	_____	_____	_____
18. May we receive a copy of your written hazard assessment criteria and procedures required by the OSHA Standard? Please attach.	_____	_____	_____

APPENDIX 3D

SAMPLE DATA BASE FORMAT

Chemical/Product Information

NAME	CAS NUMBER
SYNONYMS	FAMILY
STRUCTURAL FORMULA	PRODUCT
PRODUCT CLASS	PURITY
FORMULA	
SOLVENT	SOLVENT%
ODOR	
APPEARANCE	
COLOR	
SPECIFIC GRAVITY @20 DEG C	
SPECIFIC GRAVITY @25 DEG C	
REFRACTIVE INDEX @20 DEG C	
VISCOSITY CPS @25 DEG C	
MELTING POINT [C]	
BOILING POINT [C]	
CONGEALING POINT [C]	
FREEZING POINT [C]	
VAPOR PRESSURE (MG/HG)	
VAPOR DENSITY [AIR = 1]	
PERCENT VOLATILE	
EVAPORATION RATE	
SOLUBILITY-WATER	
SOLUBILITY-OIL	
SOLUBILITY-OTHER	MOL.WT.
PH	

MAJOR 5 HAZARDOUS CONSTITUENTS

1ST	CAS#	PERCENT
2ND	CAS#	PERCENT
3RD	CAS#	PERCENT
4TH	CAS#	PERCENT
5TH	CAS#	PERCENT

Flammability Data

PERCENT HAZARD   AUTOIGNITION PT [F]

FLASHPOINT [F][TCC/COC]   FASHPOINT [C][TCC/COC]
LOWER FLAMMABILITY LIMIT [%]   UPPER FLAM. LIMIT [%]
LOWER EXPLOSIVE LIMIT [%]   UPPER EXPL. LIMIT [%]
FIRE CLASS [A,B,C,D]   EXTINGUISHER TYPE
SPECIAL FIRE-FIGHTING PROCEDURES

UNUSUAL FIRE & EXPLOSION HAZARDS

DECOMPOSITION PRODUCTS
AVOID THE FOLLOWING

Health Data

OVEREXPOSURE SYMPTOMS   EMERGENCY PHONE [DAY]
TLV AIR
TLV SKIN   EMERGENCY PHONE [NIGHT]
TLV ORAL

AIR ODOR THRESHOLD LEVEL (AOTL)
ODOR SAFETY FACTOR [RATIO OF TLV/AOTL]
FIRST AID

MEDICAL CONDITIONS AGGRAVATED BY

ACUTE TOXICITY
ORAL INGESTION
PRIMARY EYE IRRITATION
PRIMARY SKIN IRRITATION
DERMAL
SENSITIZATION
INHALATION
CHRONIC TOXICITY
OVEREXPOSURE EYES
OVEREXPOSURE SKIN
OVEREXPOSURE INGESTION
OVEREXPOSURE INHALATION

Spill, Leak, Disposal & Environmental Data

PRIORITY POLLUTANT?
INCINERATION [Y/N]   DISPERSAL OF WATER [Y/N]
OCEAN DUMPING [Y/N]   OPEN DISPOSAL [Y/N]
SANITARY LANDFILL [Y/N]   CHEMICAL LANDFILL [Y/N]
DEEP WELL SUBSURFACE [Y/N] SPECIAL DISPOSAL [Y/N]
UNDETERMINED [Y/N]

SPILL CONTAINMENT

PICKUP & REMOVAL PROCEDURES

AQUATIC TOXICITY

BIOCHEMICAL DEGRADABILITY DATA

OCTANOL/WATER PARTITION COEFFICIENT

GOVERNMENT REPORTING PHONE #

Protective Measures

PROTECT EYES WITH
PROTECT HANDS WITH
PROTECT SKIN WITH
PROTECT LUNGS BY USING
PROTECT CONTAINER BY
EMPTY CONTAINER CODE
TYPE OF VENTILATION
TYPE OF EMERGENCY WASH

Reactivity & Storage Specifications

IS PRODUCT STABLE?

WILL HAZARDOUS POLYMERIZATION OCCUR?

PRODUCT IS INCOMPATIBLE WITH

CONDITIONS TO AVOID

RECOMMENDED STORAGE PROCEDURES

RECOMMENDED CONTAINER

SECURITY PRECAUTIONS

Transportation Data

DOT/IMO #	UN/NA #	EPA CLASS
DOT NAME		DOT FREIGHT CLASS

FLASHPOINT [CLOSED CUP-DEG F]
COEFFICIENT OF EXPANSION
LBS/GAL AT 60 DEG F
PRECAUTIONARY LABEL REQUIRED [Y/N]
PRECAUTIONARY PLACARD [Y/N]

these diverse regulations, we request that you send this information for each material purchased from you by (*name of your school or college*). (Please indicate "N/A," Not Applicable, or "D/U," Data Unavailable, in spaces, if necessary, rather than leaving blanks.)

If you have any questions regarding this material, or our RTK policies/procedures, please contact (*name of responsible individual*) at (*telephone number*). Your completed forms should reference (*name of your school or college*) and be mailed to :

(*Name and Title*)
(*Department, School/College*)
(*Street Address*)
(*City, State, Zip Code*)
(*Telephone*)

Please notify (*name of responsible individual*) within 7 days if your completed form will not be available to us within 30 days.

Your expeditious assistance in this matter is appreciated.

Very truly yours,

(*Name*)
(*Title*)

Enclosures: Hazard Communications Data Requirements
                Supplemental Supplier Questionnaire
cc:

APPENDIX 3B

HAZARD COMMUNICATION DATA REQUIREMENTS

1. **CHEMICAL IDENTITY:** Chemical, Common and Trade Names; CAS No.; Mixture or Single Material

2. **PHYSICAL/ CHEMICAL PROPERTIES:** Water Solubility, Vapor Pressure, Flash point, Specific Gravity, Boiling Point, Volatility, Appearance, and Color

3. **PHYSICAL HAZADS:** Fire, Explosivity, Reactivity

4. **HEALTH HAZARDS:** Acute and Chronic Effects, Animal and Human Test Results, Symptoms of Exposure, Medical Conditions Aggravated by, Registry of Toxic Effects of Chemical Substances (RTECS) Data Summation, Listed by OSHA/NTP/IARC

5. **ROUTES OF ENTRY:** OSHA and ACGIH Threshold Limit Values (TLVs), Exposure Mechanisms

APPENDIX 3A
SAMPLE SUPPLIER SURVEY LETTER

(*This letter should be sent on your letterhead to all suppliers of chemicals and products for every department in your school or college.*)

Dear _____:

    (*Name of your school or college*) is currently implementing procedures that will assure our full compliance with either our state right-to-know (RTK) law or the OSHA Hazard Communication Standard. As you are probably aware, these regulations require us to make data and assessments available to our employees. In the past, we understand that many organizations made material safety data sheets (MSDSs) available for this purpose. However, detailed data and assessment requirements in federal and many state regulations encompass information not previously required in MSDSs (e.g., CAS Registry Numbers, chronic health data summaries, medical conditions aggravated by exposure, etc.). In fact, we understand that OSHA officially discontinued use of their two-page MSDS, or OSHA Form-20, several years ago because of these more extensive data requirements.

    The attached table (*use Appendix 3B*) summarizes the composite information required by federal and state hazard communication regulations. In addition, however, we must also comply with a variety of other local, state, and federal regulations. Consequently, we would appreciate your assistance in providing us with as much technical and regulatory information as possible. To aid you with our request, we have attached a Supplemental Supplier Questionnaire (*use Appendix 3C*) that will provide information we currently anticipate will be essential to our hazard communication program. To assure our full compliance with et can be used to verify that the MSDSs fulfill OSHA or applicable state right-to-know requirements.

The *Data Base Format* in this Appendix will be useful primarily to those schools and colleges that plan to computerize their hazardous chemical or product information. This particular format includes data that fulfill OSHA and all state right-to-know data requirements. The *Material Safety Data Sheets* section and the *Sample MSDS Format* illustrate the content and scope of information that should be included in MSDSs sent by your suppliers.

Supplier Information

DIVISION/PLANT

STREET ADDRESS

CITY   STATE   ZIP

MAIN PHONE #   EMERGENCY NIGHT PHONE #

Regulatory Data

OSHA REGS
DOT REGS
EPA REGS
FDA REGS
USDA REGS
CPSC REGS
LOCAL REGS

APPENDIX 3E
MATERIAL SAFETY DATA SHEETS (MSDSs)

Material safety data sheets (MSDSs) are forms on which pertinent information for a chemical or a product are recorded. Prior to promulgation of the OSHA Hazard Communication Standard, OSHA developed an MSDS format commonly known as the OSHA Form-20. This was a two-page, standardized document designed for manufacturer communication of very brief, highly summarized product information to purchasers. The extensive, detailed product information required by the OSHA Standard, however, rendered the informational content of the OSHA Form-20 obsolete. As a result, OSHA formally announced in 1985 that the OSHA Form-20 was being discontinued since it could not provide the required information. Consequently, every chemical manufacturer, supplier, and formulator must design an MSDS that incorporates the new, detailed data requirements (see Appendix 3B for details). Rather than develop another standardized format, OSHA has chosen to leave the format design to each individual manufacturer or distributor. As a general rule, if your suppliers provide you with a two-page MSDS, you can reasonably assume that they have not adequately researched, compiled, and reviewed all of the information required by the OSHA Standard.

MSDSs fulfill several functions. First and most important, the MSDS informs administrators, supervisors, and employees about chemical hazards, safe handling procedures, and proper protective equipment. Second, the MSDS provides the basis for proper container labeling. Finally, the MSDS gives critical information to community services that may be needed for emergency support (health, fire, and police departments).

MSDSs contain a number of sections. Because the headings of the sections, and their sequence, may differ slightly from supplier to supplier, we cannot possibly identify every specific heading. Information associated with the following general headings, however, should appear in some form on all MSDSs:

PRODUCT INFORMATION

The chemical name, common name, and any applicable code numbers are usually provided along with the supplier's name, address, and emergency telephone number.

HAZARDOUS INGREDIENTS (COMPOSITION DATA)

The chemical name and percentages of all hazardous ingredients are listed in this section. Other chemicals may also be listed. The Threshold Limit Value (TLV), the safe exposure limit used or recommended by the American Conference of Governmental Industrial Hygienists (ACGIH), or by the chemical manufacturer, is included in this section for the approximately 375 chemicals with existing TLVs. This numerical value represents the limit above which exposure may become hazardous.

PHYSICAL AND CHEMICAL DATA

Specific information concerning the chemical and/or the physical properties of the material is provided in this section. Many of the chemical terms used here will need to be explained in your school or college training program (written and/or oral).

FIRE AND EXPLOSION HAZARD DATA

Information in this section will help minimize the potential for a fire or explosion. In case of an unforeseeable emergency, fire-fighting procedures are also described. The flash point, if applicable, is recorded in this section, and proper fire-extinguishing media are listed.

HEALTH HAZARD DATA (PHYSIOLOGICAL EFFECTS)

Acute and chronic effects of exposure must be listed. This information alerts you to potential health hazards and defines treatments for minimizing effects of accidental exposures. First aid and emergency treatment procedures are usually also outlined in this section. Many older MSDSs contain only first aid and emergency treatment procedures, rather than the currently required acute and chronic health data. Obviously, these older MSDSs are no longer acceptable. This section should also include medical conditions aggravated by exposure.

REACTIVITY DATA

This section alerts you to chemical interaction conditions that should be avoided when handling or storing a material.

SPILL OR LEAKAGE PROCEDURES (ENVIRONMENTAL DATA)

Guidelines for the cleanup and management of emergencies that may arise, and methods for proper disposal of the material, are described in this section.

SPECIAL PROTECTIVE EQUIPMENT

This section identifies the proper protective equipment, if any, that you must wear or use when handling the material. This information should be presented to employees through written and/or verbal training.

SPECIAL PRECAUTIONS

Guidelines for the content of warnings or labels that should appear on containers of materials are listed in this section. Special hazards are highlighted, and proper handling procedures are identified.

APPENDIX 3F

SAMPLE MSDS FORMAT

MATERIAL SAFETY DATA SHEET   A-1 Chemical Manufacturer
                                                       The Synthesis Building
To Help You Handle   1234 Cork Street
This Product Safely!!   Anytown, USA 11111
                                                        (111) 111-1111

SAF-T-CIRCLE

HEALTH 2-3   FIRE 4
REACTIVITY 2   ENVIRONMENT 1-2-0
SPECIAL 0
HAZARD SUMMARY SCALE = 0 MIN. - 4 MAX.

COMMON NAME: ACETALDEHYDE
CAS NUMBER: 75-07-0   **OUR PRODUCT NUMBER:** A9012
SYNONYMS: Acetic Aldehyde, Ethyl Aldehyde, Ethanal
FORMULA: CH3CHO
CHEMICAL FAMILY: Aldehyde M1 Aliphatic Primary
EMERGENCY PHONE NUMBER BUSINESS HOURS:
     1-800-111-1111
SPEAK WITH: Safety Department
EMERGENCY PHONE NUMBER OTHER TIMES:
     1-800-111-1111
SPEAK WITH: Plant Manager

If First Aid Is Required

In case of contact, immediately flush eyes and skin with plenty of water for at least 15 minutes. Remove contaminated clothing and shoes. Call a physician. Wash clothing before reuse. Destroy contaminated shoes.

Hazardous Ingredients

HAZARDOUS MATERIALS	CAS NUMBER	% HAZARD
Acetaldehyde	75-07-0	99+

Fire and Explosion Hazards

EXTINGUISHING AGENTS RECOMMENDED: CO2, Dry Chemical
FLASH POINT (FAHRENHEIT): -36 deg (Closed Cup)
FLAMMABILITY LIMITS IN AIR (% BY VOLUME):
LOWER: 4%   **UPPER:** 57%
AUTOIGNITION WILL OCCUR AT: 347 deg F
SPECIAL FIRE-FIGHTING PROCEDURES:
Explosion-Resistant Barriers Should Be Used.
Use Self-Contained Breathing Apparatus.
UNUSUAL FIRE & EXPLOSION HAZARDS:
Severe - Vapors Explosive. Volatilizes at 69 deg F
DECOMPOSITION PRODUCTS: Not Predictable
AVOID THE FOLLOWING: Water, Heat, Open Flame

Health Hazard Data

OVEREXPOSURE EFFECTS: Eye & Local Irritant
INHALATION: LCLo (Rat) 4000 ppm/4 Hr
EYES: 40 mg (Rabbit) Severe; 50 ppm (Human) for 15 Minutes.
INGESTION: Can Cause Death, Resembles Alcoholism.
LD50 RAT = 1930 mg/kg
SKIN: 500 mg (Rabbit) Open Cup = Mild
TLV IN AIR: 100 ppm (ACGIH) **TLV SKIN:** N/R
TLV ORAL: N/R   **STEL:** 150 ppm; 270 mg/m3

AIR ODOR THRESHOLD LEVEL (AOTL): 0.05 ppm
ODOR SAFETY FACTOR (RATIO OF TLV-AIR/AOTL): 2000

Reactivity Data

PRODUCT IS: Very Unstable
CHEMICALS AND CONDITIONS TO AVOID: Acid Anhydrides, Alcohols, Ketones, Phenols, Halogens, Strong Alkalis, Isocyanates
HAZARDOUS POLYMERIZATION: Easily, To Paraldehyde
HAZARDOUS DECOMPOSITION: Heat, Oxygen, Ammonia, Hydrogen Sulfide

Spill, Leak, and Waste Disposal Procedures

REPORT ALL LEAKS AND SPILLS TO APPROPRIATE GOVERNMENTAL AGENCY
PRECAUTIONARY MEASURES: Keep Away from Heat, Sparks, Flame. Keep Container Closed. Use with Adequate Ventilation. Wash Throughly After Handling.
STOP SPILL AT SOURCE IF POSSIBLE. Dike Large Quantities.
PICKUP & REMOVAL: Absorb with Vermiculite and Place in a Covered Container.

INCINERATION: Yes	**DISPERSAL TO WATER:** No
OCEAN DUMPING: No	**LAGOON:** No
SANITARY CHEMICAL LANDFILL: No	**LANDFILL:** No

DEEP WELL SUBSURFACE: No **OPEN DISPOSAL:** No
UNDETERMINED DISPOSAL: Quantity-Dependent
PRIORITY POLLUTANT (IF CHECKED): No

Personal Protection and Hygiene Information

PERSONAL HYGIENE PRACTICES MUST INCLUDE: After Handling Wash Hands and Face.
PROTECT YOUR EYES WITH: Full Face Shield

PROTECT YOUR HANDS BY USING: Neoprene Gloves
PROTECT YOUR SKIN BY USING: Apron
PROTECT YOUR BREATHING BY USING: Ventilation,
Cartridge Respirator or Air-Supplied Respirator
SAF-T-LABEL PROTECTIVE EQUIPEMENT SYMBOLS: 1, 2,
4, 9, 11

Storage and Containers

SPECIAL PRECAUTIONS: Highly Reactive—DANGEROUS
RECOMMENDED CONTAINERS: Isolated Flammable Liquid
Containers, Cabinet, and Room
PROTECT THE CONTAINER BY: Grounding, Ventilation, Cool
Storage Area
CONTAINER SHOULD BE HANDLED IN AREA WITH:
Ventilation Hood
THE EMPTY CONTAINER IS: Explosive, Flammable

Precautionary Label

IS A PRECAUTIONARY LABEL REQUIRED? Yes
IS A WARNING PLACARD REQUIRED? Yes
DOT/IMO # 3.1 **UN/NA #** 1089
HAZARD CLASSIFICATION: Flammable Liquid, Hazard
Rating = 3
DOT NAME: Acetaldehyde
SHIPPING INSTRUCTIONS: Keep Away from Heat, Sparks,
Flame. Keep Container Closed. Use with Adequate
Ventilation. Wash Thoroughly After Handling.
PLACARD WARNINGS: Warning Flammable

Environmental Risks

AQUATIC TOXICITY: N/R
DEGRADABILITY - In Water
Photolysis in Air (Atmospheric Residence
Time = 0.03 - 0.07 Days)
PARTITION COEFFICIENT: N/I

Regulatory References

REFER TO THE FOLLOWING REFERENCES:
OSHA REGULATIONS: 29 CFR 1910.1000
DOT REGULATIONS: 49 CFR
EPA REGULATIONS: N/R
OTHER: N/I

Physical Data

ODOR: Pungent, Green, Fruity, Ethereal
APPEARANCE: Fuming Liquid
COLOR: Colorless
MOLECULAR WEIGHT: 44.05
SPECIFIC GRAVITY AT 20 DEG C: 0.804-0.811
REFRACTIVE INDEX AT 20 DEG C: 1.3392
VISCOSITY CPS @ 25 DEG C: N/I
MELTING POINT [C]: -123.5(-121)
BOILING POINT [C]: 20.8
CONGEALING POINT [C]: N/I
FREEZING POINT [C]: -123.5
VAPOR PRESSURE [MM/HG]: 740 mm
VAPOR DENSITY [AIR = 1]: 1.52
PERCENT VOLATILE: 100
EVAPORATION RATE: N/R
SOLUBILITY IN WATER: Miscible
SOLUBILITY IN ALCOHOL: All Proportions
SOLUBILITY IN OIL: All Proportions
SOLUBILITY OTHER: Broad

SIGNATURE: **TITLE:**

DATE:

THE INFORMATION PRESENTED HEREIN RELATES TO THE
SPECIFIC MATERIAL DESCRIBED AND MAY NOT BE VALID
FOR THIS MATERIAL USED IN COMBINATION WITH ANY
OTHER MATERIALS OR IN ANY PROCESS. THIS

INFORMATION IS, WE BELIEVE TO THE BEST OF OUR
KNOWLEDGE, ACCURATE AND RELIABLE ON THE DATE
COMPILED. WE MAKE NO REPRESENTATION, WARRANTY,
OR GUARANTEE AS TO ITS ACCURACY, RELIABILITY, OR
COMPLETENESS. IT IS THE READER'S RESPONSIBILITY
TO ASCERTAIN WHETHER THE INFORMATION SUPPLIED
IS SUITABLE AND COMPLETE FOR THAT PERSON'S
SPECIFIC USES.

N/A = NOT APPLICABLE
N/R = NOT REPORTED
N/I = NOT INDICATED

APPENDIX 4

HAZARD ASSESSMENT CRITERIA

OSHA regulations require that your school or college define your hazard assessment criteria in writing, and make these criteria available to employees and to OSHA inspectors. This Appendix consists of written acute health, chronic health, fire, and reactivity/explosivity hazard assessment criteria that have been compiled and adapted by FSE from several independent sources. Utilization of these by your school or college will fulfill federal and state requirements for written criteria and enable you to provide your employees semi-quantitative hazard ratings, either in training materials or on in-house labels.

The OSHA Hazard Assessment Criteria, the National Fire Protection Association (NFPA) Hazard Assessment Criteria, and American National Standards Institute (ANSI) Standards for Hazardous Chemicals are summarized in the tables that follow. Numerous other hazard assessment criteria are also available, but we did not find them compatible with integration into the semi-quantitative system presented in this Appendix.

APPENDIX 4A

ACUTE TOXICITY RATING CRITERIA*

Acute Toxicity Rating	ORAL** Liquids, Solids LD50 Rat (mg/kg)	DERMAL Liquids, Solids LD50 Rabbit (mg/kg)	SKIN IRRITATION Gases, Vapors (ppm), Dusts, Fumes, Mists (mg/l) LC50 Rat 1 Hour Exposure	INHALATION Liquids, Solids Skin Irritation 4 Hour Exposure***	EYE IRRITATION Liquids, Solids Eye Irritation
4	<1	<20	<0.2 mg/l <20 ppm	Corrosive Extremely irritating	Corrosive Irreversible corneal opacity
3	1–50	20–200	0.2–2 mg/l >20–200 ppm	Severely irritating Persisting >7 days	Severely irritating and persisting >7 days Reversible corneal opacity
2	50–500	200–1,000	2–20 mg/l >200–2,000 ppm	Primary or moderate irritant Sensitizer Reversible within 7 days	Moderately irritating but reversible within 7 days
1	500–5,000	1,000–5,000	20–200 mg/l >2,000–10,000 ppm	Slightly irritating	Slightly irritating but reversible within 7 days
0	5,000	5,000	200 mg/l >10,000 ppm	Essentially nonirritating	Essentially nonirritating

* Adapted from the National Paint & Coatings Association Revised HMIS Rating Manual.
** The oral route of exposure is less likely in a workplace setting. If situations are encountered where the oral LD50 value would indicate a significantly different rating, however, toxicity values for the other routes of entry may be considered more appropriate when assigning the rating.
*** Usually tested in rabbits. Note animal species and duration of exposure if different.

APPENDIX 4B

CHRONIC TOXICITY RATING CRITERIA FOR ROUTES OF POTENTIAL HUMAN EXPOSURE

Hazard Rating	Organ Effects	Reproductive Effects	Carcinogenicity	Environmental Persistence*
4	Significant life-threatening effects documented in humans.	Confirmed human effects (NIOSH, OSHA publications).	Confirmed human carcinogen (OSHA, IARC publications).	Highly persistent carcinogens, mutagens, and/or reproductive toxins.
3	Suspected human effects and/or estimated life-threatening effects in >2 animal species at exposure levels <5× expected human exposure.	Suspected human effects and/or animal effects in >2 species at exposure levels >3× expected human exposure.	Suspected human carcinogen. Tentative human evidence possibly supported by animal data.	Highly persistent.
2	Significant, not life-threatening effects in >2 animal species. No significant human effects known.	Animal effects in >2 species at 3–10× expected human exposure. No significant human effects known.	Animal carcinogen in >2 species. No significant human effects known.	Persistent.
1	Animal effects in 1 species. No significant human effects known.	Animal effects in 1 species. No significant human effects known.	Animal carcinogen in 1 species and/or effects in >3 in vitro mutagenicity assays. No significant human effects known.	Somewhat persistent.
0	No significant effects in animals or humans.	No significant effects in animals or humans.	No significant effects in animals or humans.	Nonpersistent. Easily biodegradable.

* After 40 CFR 300, Appendix A, Table 5.

APPENDIX 4C

PHYSICAL HAZARD ASSESSMENT CRITERIA*

Hazard Rating	Flammability Hazard	Reactivity Hazard
4	Gases, cryogenic materials, and liquids that rapidly vaporize at ambient temperature and pressure and form explosive mixtures with air; dust of combustible solids: Flash point 73° F (23° C), and Boiling Point <100° F (38° C).	Materials readily capable of explosion at ambient temperature and pressure or from mechanical or localized thermal shock.
3	Liquids and solids that ignite spontaneously when exposed to air at ambient temperature and pressure: Flash point <73° F (23° C) and Boiling Point >100° F (38° C) or Flash point 73–100° F (23–38° C).	Unstable materials that react explosively with water, are capable of explosion when heated under confinement, or are sensitive to thermal and mechanical shock under confinement.
2	Liquids and solids that ignite only when heated moderately or exposed to high ambient temperature: Flash point 100–200° F (38–129° C).	Unstable materials that react violently with water or readily undergo violent chemical change, but do not explode.
1	Liquids and solids that will burn at <1500° F: Flashpoint >200° F (129° C) (most ordinary combustible materials).	Normally stable materials that become unstable at elevated temperature and pressure or react nonviolently with water.
0	Materials that will not burn at <1500° F (815° C).	Normally stable materials that do not react with water.

*After NFPA Identification System - Standard 704.

Note: Other unique hazards such as oxidizer, water-reactive, or radioactive will not be quantified, but will be identified in MSDSs and on labels as required by law.

APPENDIX 4D

OSHA HAZARD ASSESSMENT CRITERIA

1. HAZARDOUS CHEMICALS IDENTIFIED IN:

    OSHA (29 CFR Part 1910 Subpart Z)
    American Conference of Governmental Industrial Hygienists
      (ACGIH) Threshold Limit Values (TLVs)

2. CARCINOGENS IDENTIFIED IN:

    OSHA (29 CFR Part 1910 Subpart Z)
    National Toxicology Program (NTP) Annual Report
    International Agency for Research in Cancer (IARC) Monographs
    Registry of Toxic Effects of Chemical Substances (RTECS)

3. HAZARDOUS MIXTURES IDENTIFICATION:

    Produced adverse health effects when tested in biological essays as a
      whole
    Not tested, but adverse health effects are produced by any ingredient
      >1% (e.g., Threshold Limit Values, TLVs, exist)
    Not tested, but carcinogenic effects are produced by any ingredient
      >0.1%
    Not tested, but "available data" indicate a potential for physical
      effects (fire, reactivity, or explosivity)

4. WRITTEN SCHOOL OR COLLEGE HAZARD ASSESSMENT
    CRITERIA:

    Available for inspection by OSHA
    Included in your Written Hazard Communication Program
    Applied to mixtures created by any school or college personnel

APPENDIX 4E

NATIONAL FIRE PROTECTION ASSOCIATION (NFPA) HAZARD ASSESSMENT CRITERIA

Scale	Health	Flammability	Reactivity	Environmental	Special*
4	Short exposure causes death or major injury	Rapidly vaporizes at ambient conditions and burns readily	Spontaneously explodes at ambient conditions	Non-biodegradable with serious health hazards	
					Reacts explosively with water
3	Short exposure causes temporary or residual injury	Ignitable under almost all ambient conditions	Explodes with a strong initiating source, reacts explosively with water	Slowly biodegrades with serious health hazards	
					Oxidizer
2	Intense or continuous exposure causes temporary or possible residual injury	Ignites with moderate heating	Normally unstable and readily undergoes violent change without detonation	Slowly biodegrades with minor health hazards	
					Radiation hazard
1	Exposure causes irritation or minor residual injury	Must be preheated for ignition	Normally stable but becomes unstable at high temperatures and pressures	Moderately biodegradable with minor hazards	
0	No hazard	Will not burn	Normally stable, not reactive with water	No hazard, rapidly biodegradable	

*NFPA does not rank these Special Hazards on their assessment scale.

APPENDIX 4F

AMERICAN NATIONAL STANDARDS INSTITUTE (ANSI)
PRECAUTIONARY LABELING CRITERIA
FOR HAZARDOUS CHEMICALS AND PRODUCTS

	Segments	Options	Selected Examples
1.	Exposure/Hazard	6	Ingestion, absorption, inhalation, contact, corrosiveness, flammability
2.	Hazard Classes	14	Highly toxic, irritant (eye), corrosive, flammable liquid, strong oxidizer
3.	Signal Words	3	Danger! Warning! Caution!
4.	Hazard States	17	May be fatal if swallowed
5.	Precautionary Measures	14	Wash thoroughly after handling
6.	First Aid	10	In case of contact, immediately flush eyes with plenty of water for at least 15 minutes and call a physician
7.	Instructions	5	In case of fire, use water, spray, foam, dry chemical, or carbon dioxide

APPENDIX 5

EMPLOYEE TRAINING MANUAL OUTLINE

A. INTRODUCTION

1. Understanding "Hazards"
2. Useful Definitions
    a. Hazard Terms
    b. Physical Hazards
    c. Health Hazards

B. OSHA HAZARD COMMUNICATION STANDARD (IF APPLICABLE)

1. Written Program
2. Hazard Assessments & MSDSs
3. Labeling
4. Training
5. Manufacturer Responsibilities
6. Employer Responsibilities
7. Employee Rights

C. STATE RIGHT-TO-KNOW REQUIREMENTS (IF APPLICABLE)

1. Hazardous Substance List
2. Inventory or Audit
3. Data Sheets and Product Research
4. Label Requirements
5. Employee Education and Training

D. EMPLOYEE HEALTH AND SAFETY

1. Material Safety Data Sheets (MSDSs)
2. Warning Labels
3. Occupational Hazard Avoidance
4. Hazardous Chemical Detection Procedures
5. Exposure Levels and Durations
6. Personal Factors Affecting Chemical Exposure

E.   ENVIRONMENTAL SAFETY

  1.   Employee Work Practices
  2.   Fire and Explosion Prevention
  3.   Spill and Leak Control
  4.   Cleanup and Proper Disposal

F.   HAZARDOUS MATERIALS USED IN OUR SCHOOL OR COLLEGE

  1.   List of Hazardous Chemicals
  2.   List of Products Containing Hazardous Chemicals
  3.   Chemical Storage and Disposal Policies

G.   SUMMARY AND CONCLUSIONS

  1.   Regulatory Requirements and Procedures
  2.   Definitions and Concepts
  3.   Safety and Health Principles
  4.   MSDSs and Work Area Hazards
  5.   Hazard Chemical Detection Procedures
  6.   Protective Equipment
  7.   Emergency Responses and Procedures
  8.   School or College Policies

APPENDIX 6

EMPLOYEE SEMINAR OUTLINE

A. GENERAL POLICIES AND PROCEDURES

1. Central File Information
2. Reporting Potential Exposures
3. Health Program
4. Industrial Hygiene Evaluations
5. Engineering Controls
6. Hazard Assessment Procedures
7. Proper Handling Guidelines

B. COMMUNICATION MECHANISMS

1. Central File
2. Chemical Data Sheet Instructions
3. Labels
4. Training Manual and Meetings

C. HAZARDOUS MATERIALS (CHEMICALS AND PRODUCTS)

1. Review Specific Materials Handled Within Each Department
   a. Hazards—Safe Levels
   b. Protective Equipment—"Hands On"
   c. Proper Handling
2. Symptoms of Exposure—Data Sheets
3. Medical Conditions Aggravated by Exposure—Data Sheets
4. Methods To Detect and Prevent Exposure
   a. Industrial Hygiene
   b. Engineering
5. Emergency Procedures—"Hands On"
   a. Fire
   b. First Aid
   c. Decontamination

D.   HAZARDOUS WASTE MANAGEMENT

    1.   Designated Areas
    2.   Responsible Departments
    3.   Applicable Procedures
    4.   Regulatory Requirements

Key to Abbreviations

ACGIH	American Conference of Governmental Industrial Hygienists
ANSI	American National Standards Institute
CAS#	Chemical Abstract Service Registry Numbers assigned by the CAS
CDS	Chemical Data Sheet, created by the New York State DOH
CFR	Code of Federal Regulations
CERCLA	Comprehensive Environmental Response, Compensation and Liability Act
COC	Cleveland Open Cup flash point test procedure
CPSC	U.S. Consumer Product Safety Commission
DEP	Department of Environmental Protection
DILHR	Department of Industry, Labor and Human Relations
distr.	Distributor
DOH	Department of Health
DOL	Department of Labor
DOLI	Department of Labor and Industry
DNR	Department of Natural Resources
E&T	Education and Training
EPA	U.S. Environmental Protection Agency
FDA	U.S. Food and Drug Administration
FSE	The Forum for Scientific Excellence, Inc.
HSFS	Hazardous Substance Fact Sheet produced by the NJ DOH
IARC	International Agency for Research in Cancer, in Lyon, France
IMO	International Maritime Organization
kg	Kilograms

LD50	Lethal Dose 50 = lethal dose to 50% of a test animal population
mfr.	Manufacturer
mg/Hg	Milligrams of mercury
mg/l	Milligrams per liter
mol. wt.	Molecular weight
MSDS	Material Safety Data Sheets, provided by chemical manufacturers to employers
N.D.C.C.	North Dakota Century Code
NFPA	National Fire Protection Association, in Quincy Massachusetts
NIOSH	National Institute for Occupational Safety and Health
NTP	National Toxicology Program, in Raleigh, North Carolina
OHSSA	Oklahoma Occupational Health and Safety Standards Act
OSHA	U.S. Occupational Safety and Health Administration, in the Department of Labor
RTECS	Registry of Toxic Effects of Chemicals, published by NIOSH
RTK	Right-To-Know
SARA	Superfund Amendments Re-Authorization Act
SIC	Standard Industrial Classification Codes
TCC	Tagliabue Closed Cup flash point test procedure
TLV	Threshold Limit Values, established by ACGIH
UN/NA	United Nations/North America
USDA	U.S. Department of Agriculture
> or ≥	Greater than, or greater than or equal to
< or ≤	Less than, or less than or equal to

Series Description

CHEMICAL AND ENVIRONMENTAL SAFETY AND HEALTH IN SCHOOLS AND COLLEGES

Comprehensive Hazard Communication and Right-To-Know Compliance Publications

Now being compiled and written by The Forum For Scientific Excellence, Inc., this series is designed to facilitate school and college compliance with federal and state hazardous chemical regulations and to provide required employee training and understanding. The information contained in the series is the result of the author's extensive and ongoing consulting experience in this field.

These publications cover essentially every aspect of the OSHA Standard and individual state Right-To-Know laws, and encompass the following:

1. Policies, procedures, and administration

2. Employee training and communication

3. Hazardous chemical and product information

Policies, Procedures, and Administrative References

Compact School and College Administrator's Guide for Compliance with Federal and State Right-To-Know Regulations

Translates the "legalese" and technical language of current hazardous chemical standards and regulations into meaningful, easily understood terminology. Provides a simplified, step-by-step program to assure that an institution or system fulfills all compliance requirements. Valuable introduction for all concerned with developing a workable, effective program.

Written Hazard Communication Program for Schools and Colleges

Identifies and describes the objectives an educational institution must achieve to assure that its hazardous chemical compliance program is appropriate and adequate. Includes specific examples of the written program requirements, including the MSDS format and hazard assessment criteria, as well as communication vehicles and formats. Essential for the administrator assigned responsibility for the compliance program. Practical ring binding allows individualized inclusions of additional local information specific to the site.

Employee Training and Communication Manuals—Five-Year Program

The following texts are designed for quantity distribution and use in fulfilling the ongoing training requirement in the OSHA Standard and various state regulations. They are useful for formal in-house training programs and seminars and also are effective individual self-study tools. As a five-year program the order of presentation suggested may be changed to fit local needs, although initial use of *Volume 1: Basic Principles* is strongly recommended. Additionally, since the workforce rarely is static, concurrent use of different texts with employee subgroups is a natural outcome. All five texts fulfill federal and state ongoing training requirements. Special discounts are available on quantity orders.

Concise Manuals of Chemical and Environmental Safety in Schools and Colleges

Volume 1: Basic Principles

A comprehensive primer that provides individual employees the basic definitions, concepts, and methods for dealing with hazardous materials safely. Reviews federal and state standards and regulations and discusses MSDSs, various definitions, labeling, occupational medicine and industrial hygiene, protective equipment, and proper work practices and procedures.

Volume 2: Hazardous Chemical Classes

A second-year training and communication resource for individual employees. Expands hazardous chemical information into classes of chemical hazards, including routes of absorption, flammables, corrosives, poisons, oxidizers and reactives/explosives, radioactive materials, carcinogens, mutagens, and teratogens, as well as general human and environmental safety. Gives emergency treatment procedures for groups of hazardous chemicals within each class.

Volume 3: Chemical Interactions

Third-year training and communication text module. Describes serious, "hidden" hazards and incidents that can arise when two or more chemicals interact inappropriately. Outlines mechanisms for prevention of such unnecessary hazards.

Volume 4: Safe Chemical Storage
An essential, ready reference that identifies procedures for safely storing chemicals and products in a variety of educational areas, including laboratories, art and graphics areas, industrial and vocational shops, and custodial and storage areas. Describes severe dangers created by storing chemicals in alphabetical order. Lists chemicals that should not be present and those that become more hazardous with age.

Volume 5: Safe Chemical Disposal
A detailed description of proper procedures for safely disposing of various classes of hazardous chemicals and products in educational institutions. Identifies safe interim storage procedures and potentially hazardous chemical interactions that must be avoided. Describes mechanisms to minimize costs and assure proper regulatory compliance. Fulfills OSHA, EPA, and many state requirements.

Pocket Guides to Chemical and Environmental Safety in Schools and Colleges

Five condensed, portable "field" guides with the same volume numbers and titles as the *Concise Manuals* above. Each includes essential information and checklists found in the *Concise Manuals* but in abbreviated form with less theory and examples. Designed for quantity distribution and use; handy pocket size; quantity discounts also are available.

Hazardous Chemical and Product Information

Handbook of Chemical and Environmental Safety in Schools and Colleges

A comprehensive master reference containing all of the information presented in the five *Concise Manuals* and *Pocket Guides* described above, as well as additional regulatory data and checklists. Includes basic chemical safety and health principles, hazardous chemical classes, hazardous interactions, and safe storage and disposal procedures. A "total" sourcebook for anyone wanting substantial treatment of principles, techniques, and legal requirements.

Compendium of Hazardous Chemicals in Schools and Colleges

Encyclopedic coverage of more than 700 hazardous chemicals commonly found in schools and colleges. Includes all data necessary for properly identifying and defining the acute and chronic health hazards of each chemical, as well as fire, explosion, environmental, and special risks such as radiation or oxidation for each of the substances. Also includes actual hazard assessments derived from published hazard assessment criteria, as well as labeling data. The information fulfills all aspects of federal and state data requirements and also includes additional nonrequired information that has been found useful in managing effective programs. Provides a basis for evaluating the accuracy of supplier MSDS data, regulations, and employee concerns.

Index of Hazardous Contents of Commercial Products in Schools and Colleges

Lists hazardous components found in nearly 10,000 commercial products used in educational facilities, and includes specific component chemical identities and, whenever possible, the percentage of the total content. When used in conjunction with the *Compendium* above and the *Cross-Reference Index of Hazardous Chemicals, Synonyms, and CAS Registry Numbers*, this work provides the data needed for safe practices and compliance with the OSHA Standard and state Right-To-Know laws.

List of Lists of Worldwide Hazardous Chemicals and Environmental Pollutants

The most extensive compilation of regulated hazardous chemicals and environmental pollutants available. Includes separate lists of substances regulated by more than 25 state, federal, and international agencies, along with many of their selection criteria. Also includes a master list in both alphabetical and Chemical Abstract Service (CAS) Registry Number sequence. The first place to look to see if a substance is regulated in any major area or country.

Cross-Reference Index of Hazardous Chemicals, Synonyms, and CAS Registry Numbers

An extensive cross-reference listing of more than 40,000 synonyms for the hazardous chemicals and environmental pollutants identified in the worldwide *List of Lists* above. Represents the most comprehensive source available for properly identifying common names, chemical names, and trade names associated with those regulated chemicals. Provides a ready reference for identifying the CAS numbers for common or product names that "hide" their true chemical identity.

For ordering information, prices, and delivery please contact:
   Science Information Resource Center
   J. B. Lippincott Company
   East Washington Square
   Philadelphia, PA 19105

To discuss or suggest editorial content please contact:
   The Forum For Scientific Excellence, Inc.
   200 Woodport Road
   Sparta, NJ 07871

INDEX